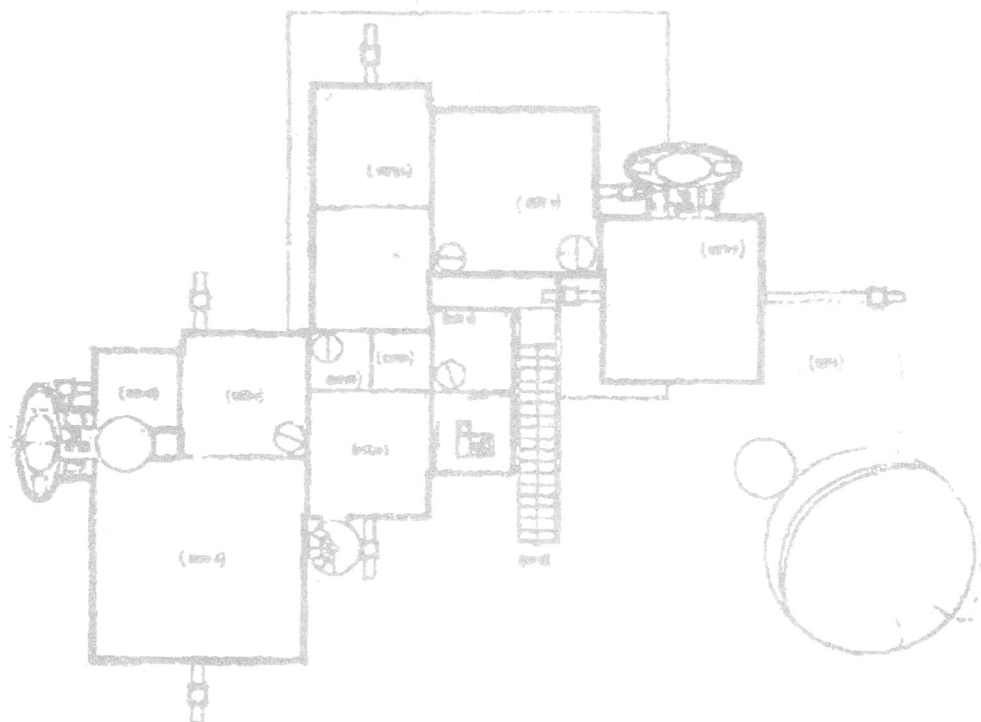

KARL LAGERFELD ■ THE HOUSE IN THE TREES

Steidl

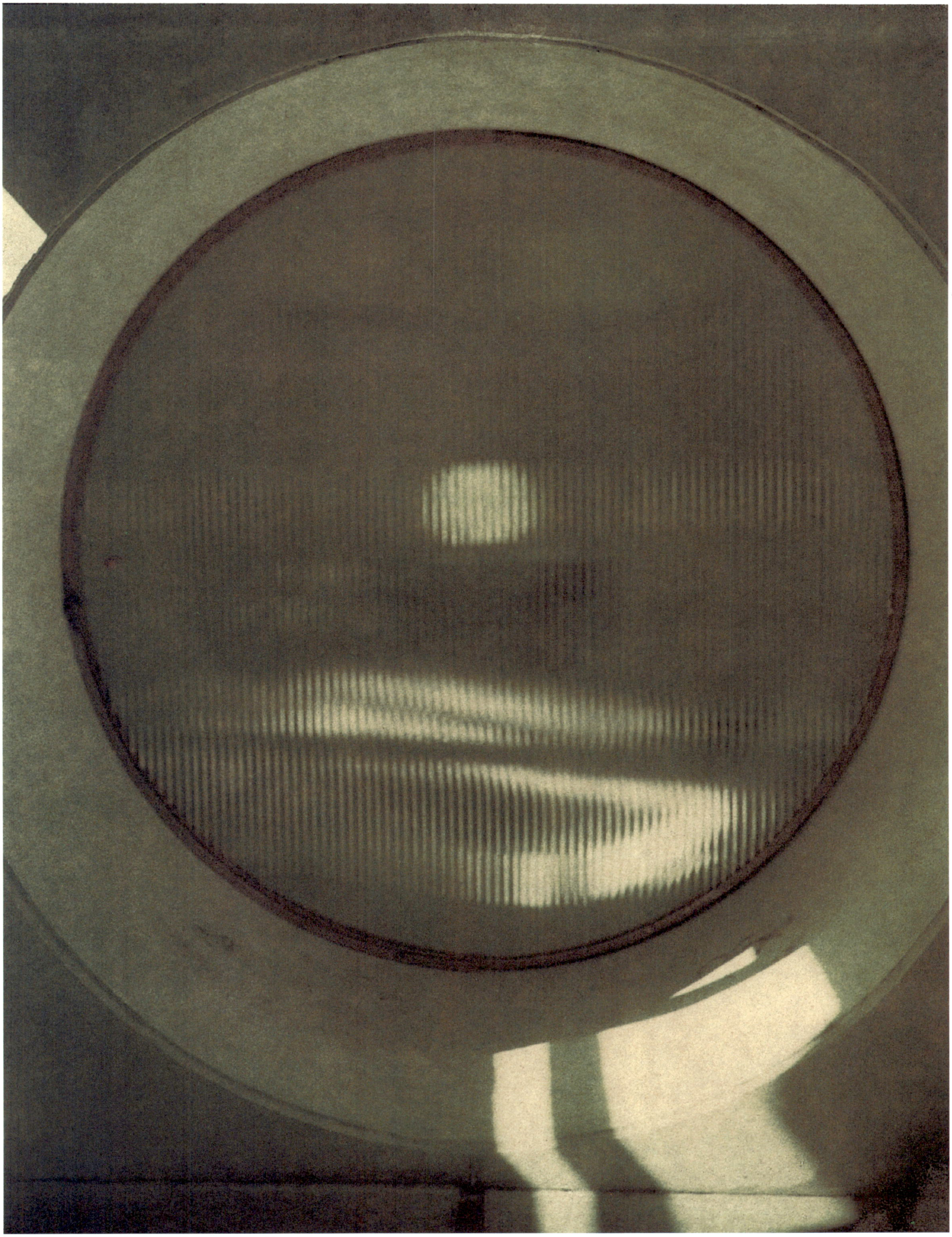

For

Uga de Plaisant in Perugini

I

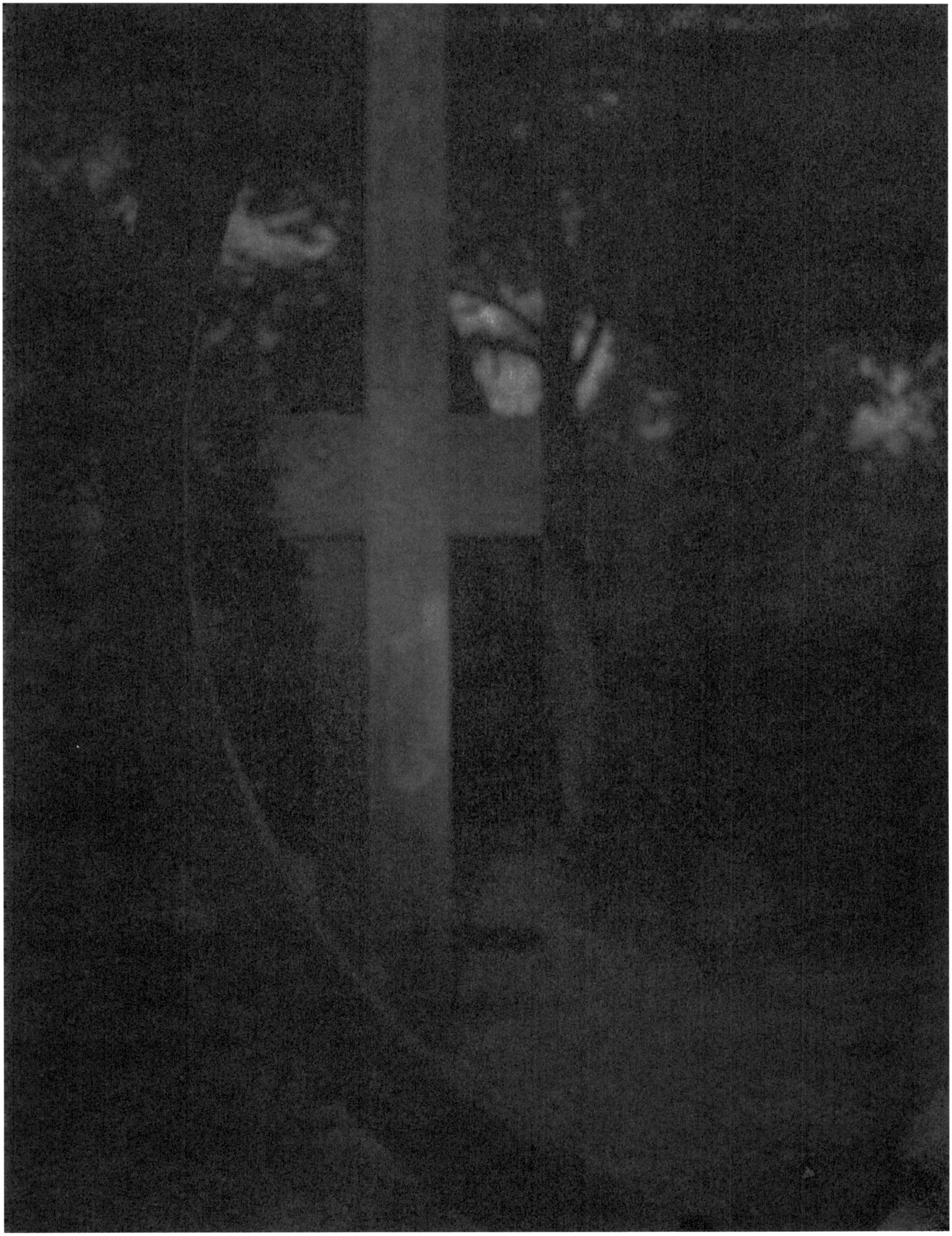

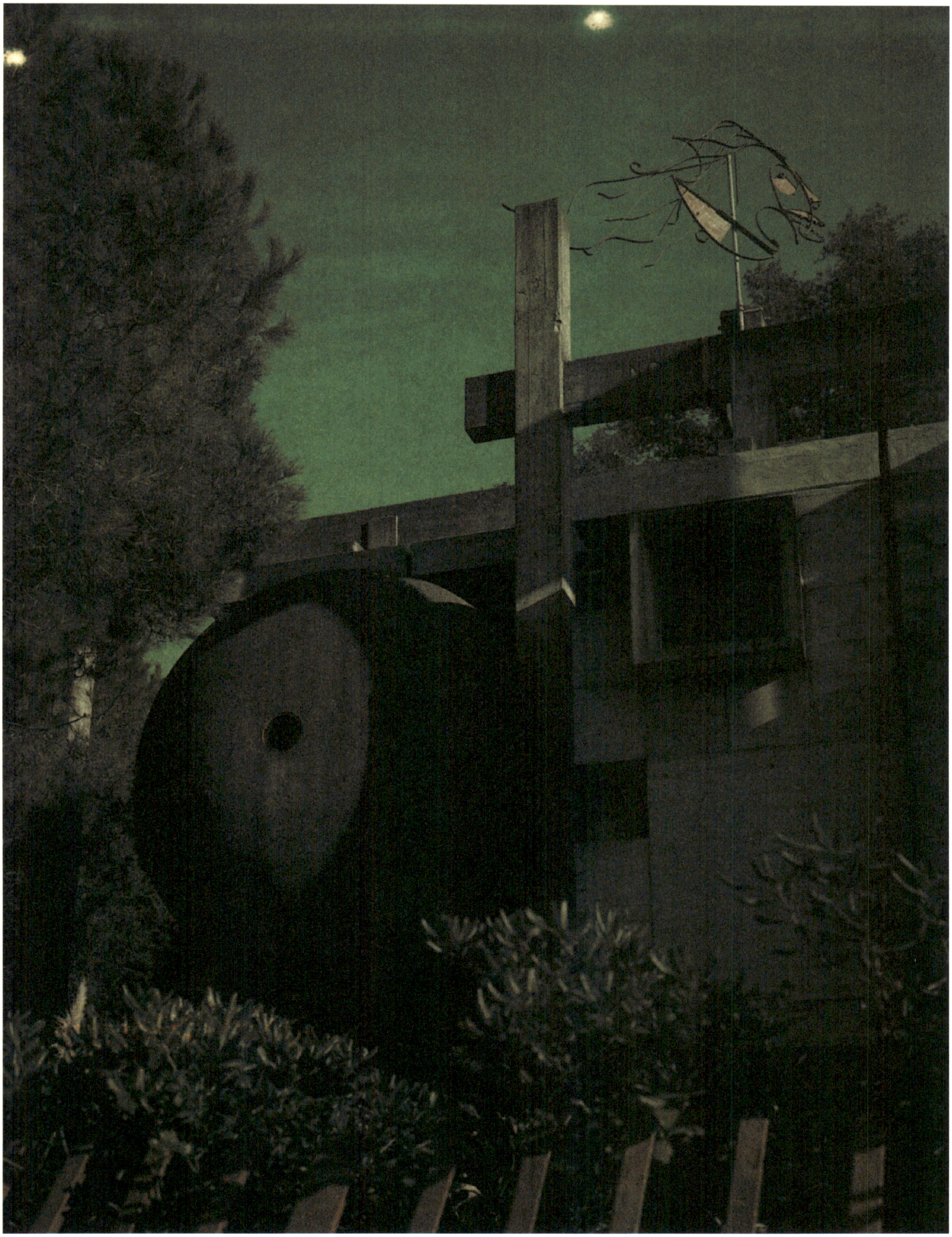

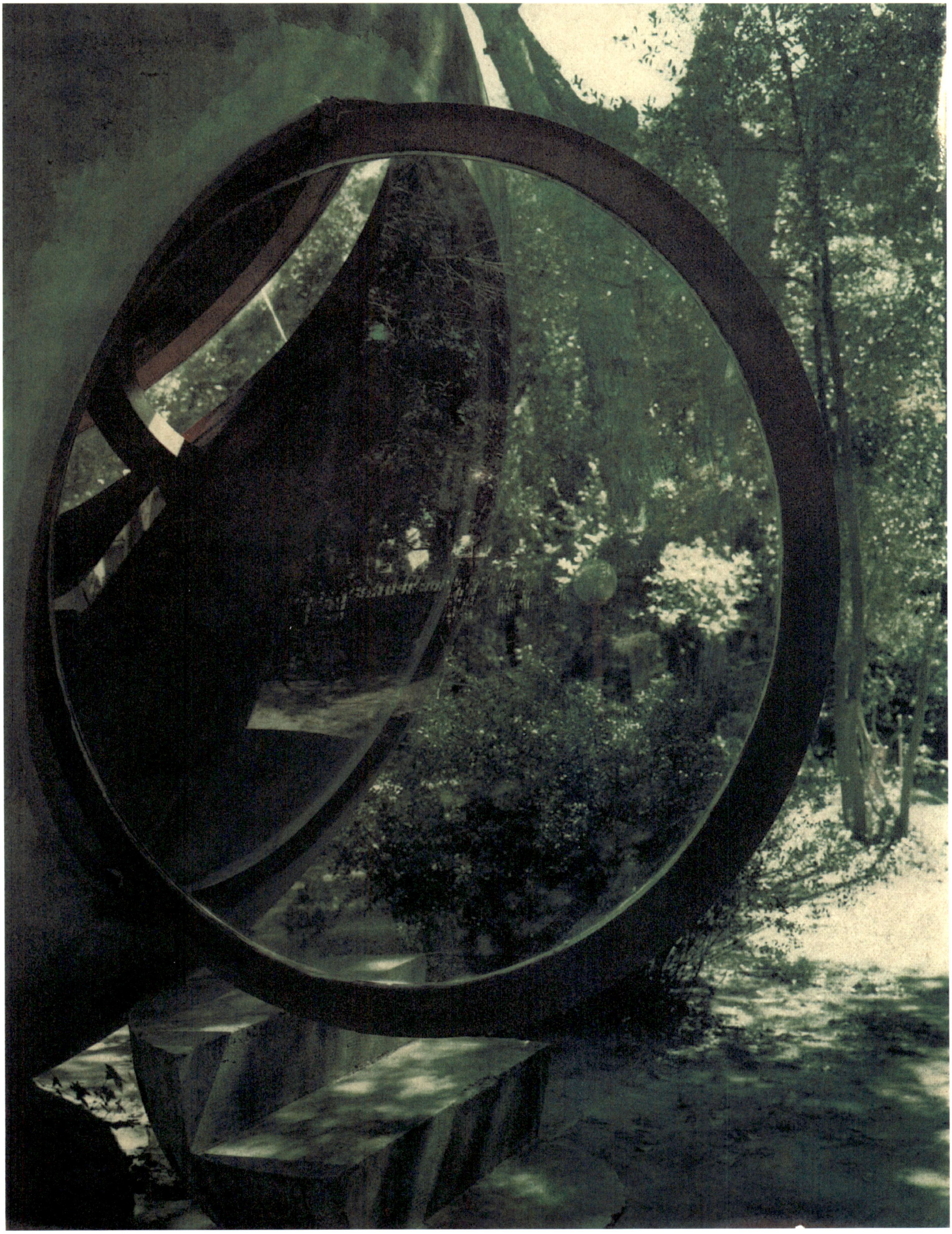

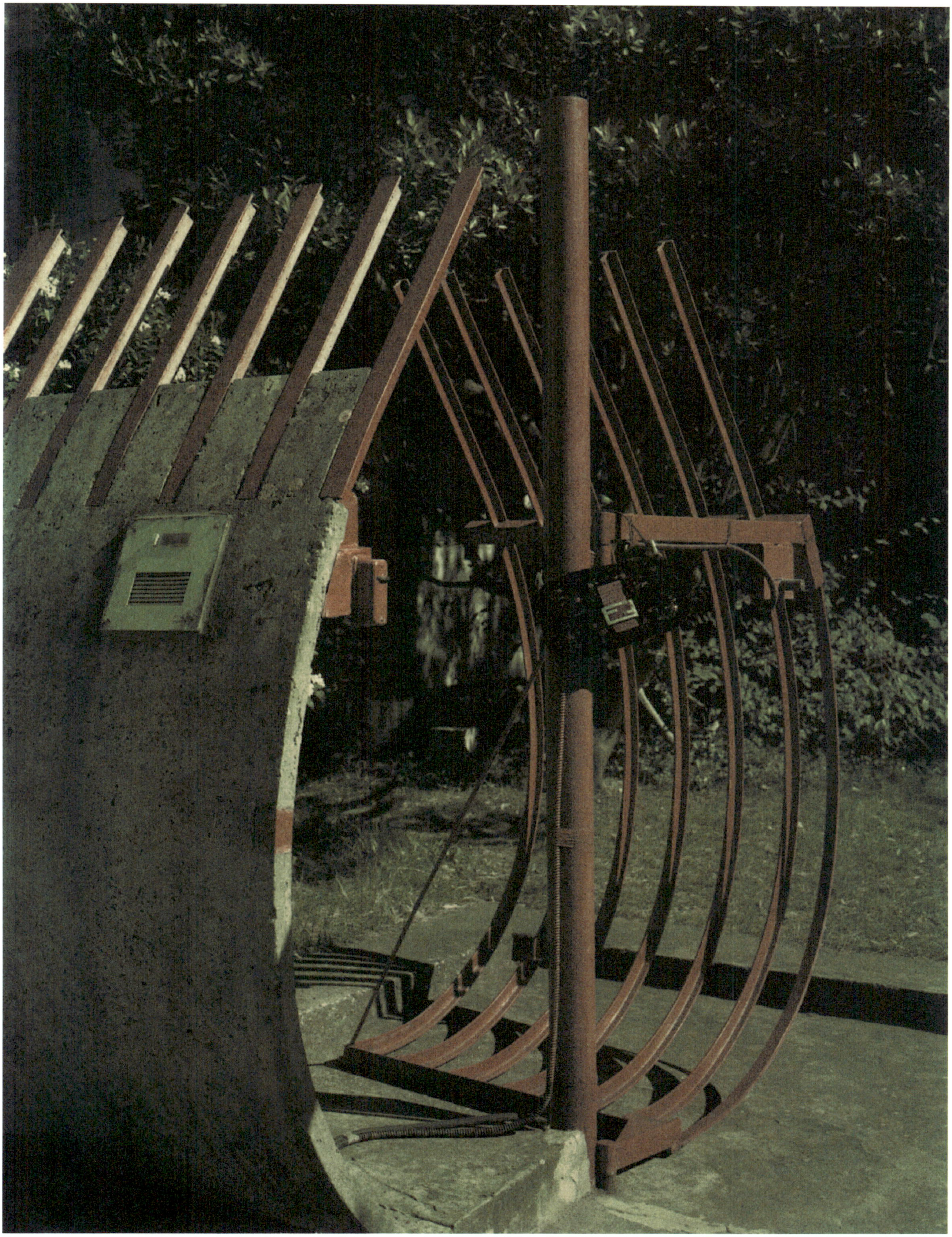

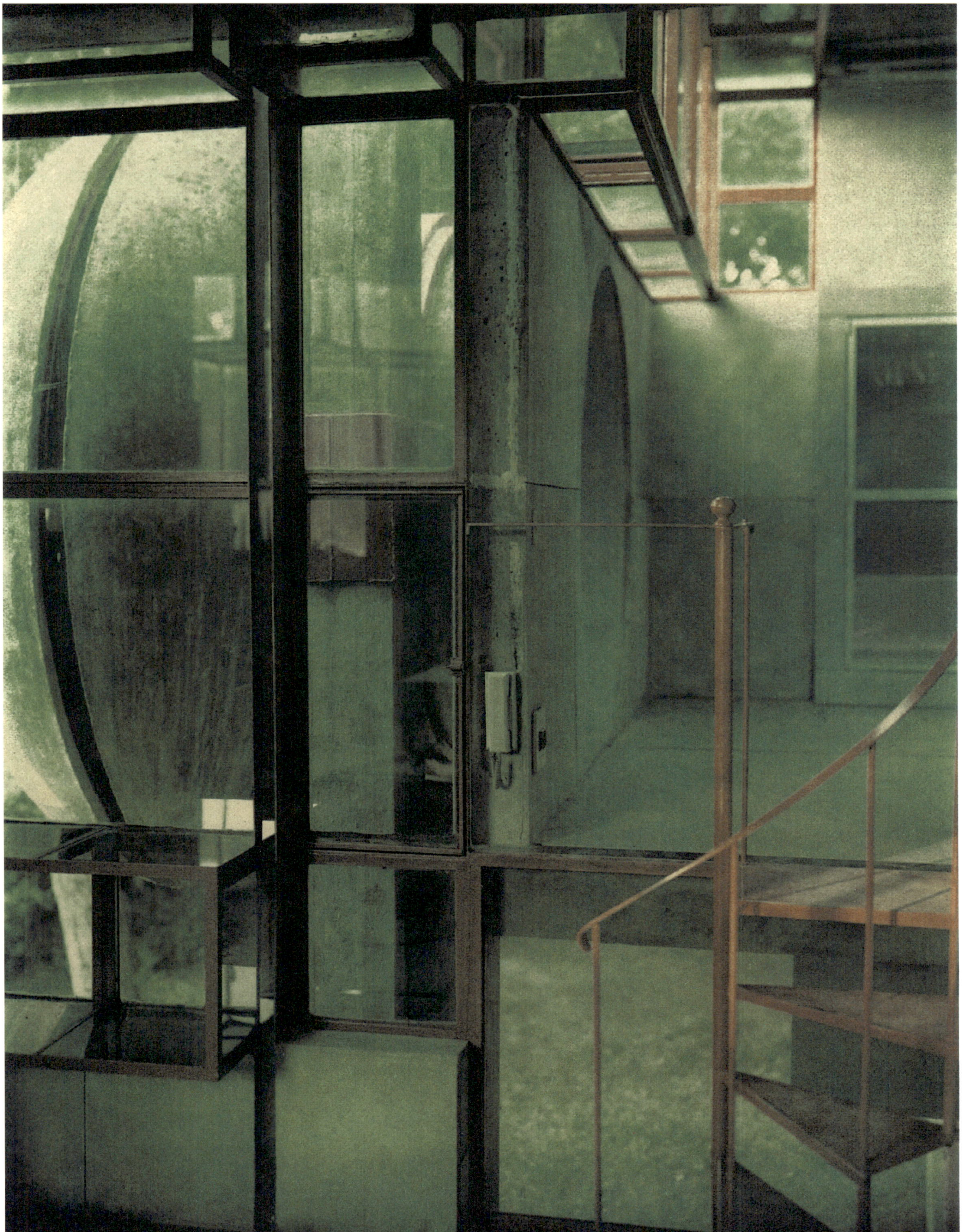

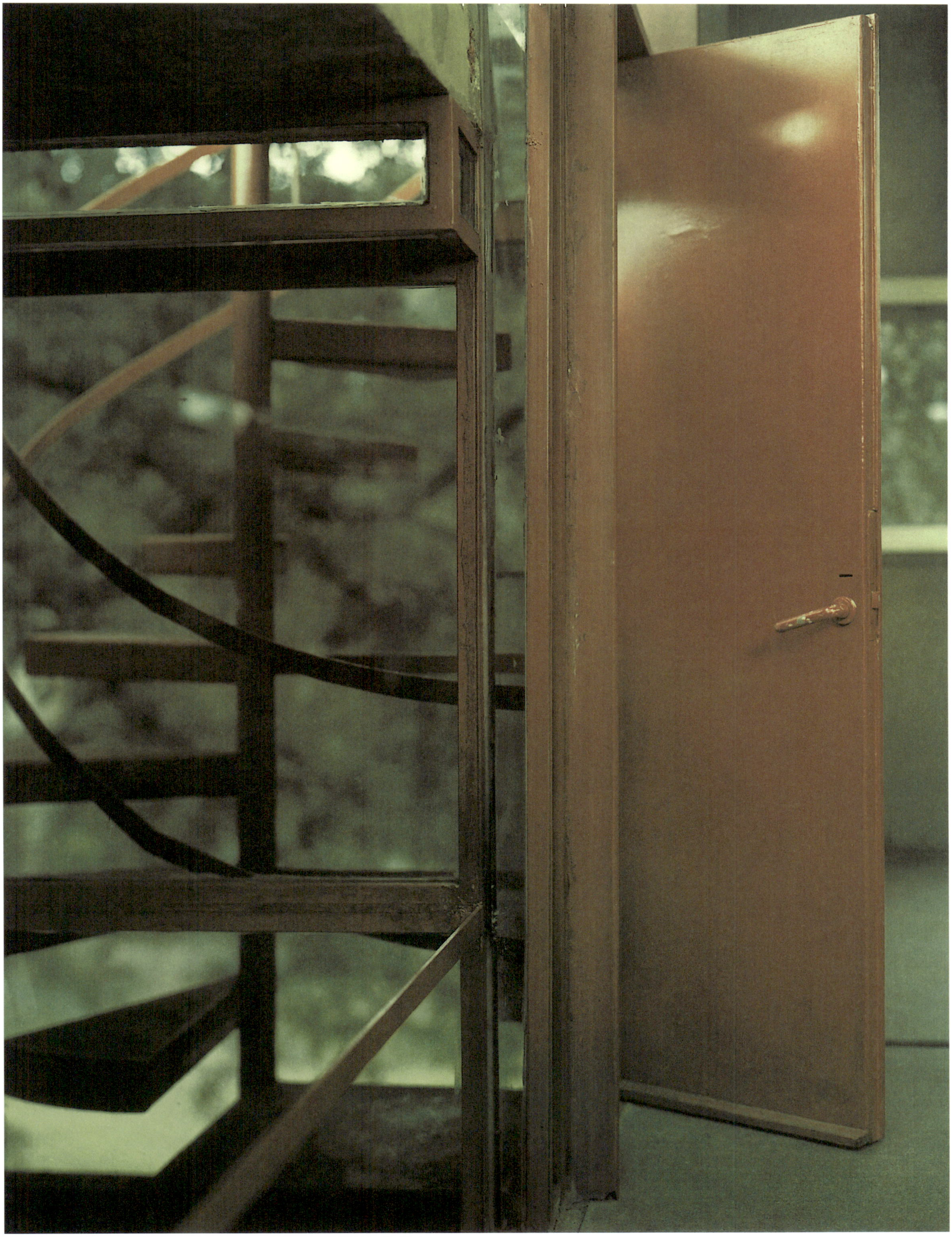

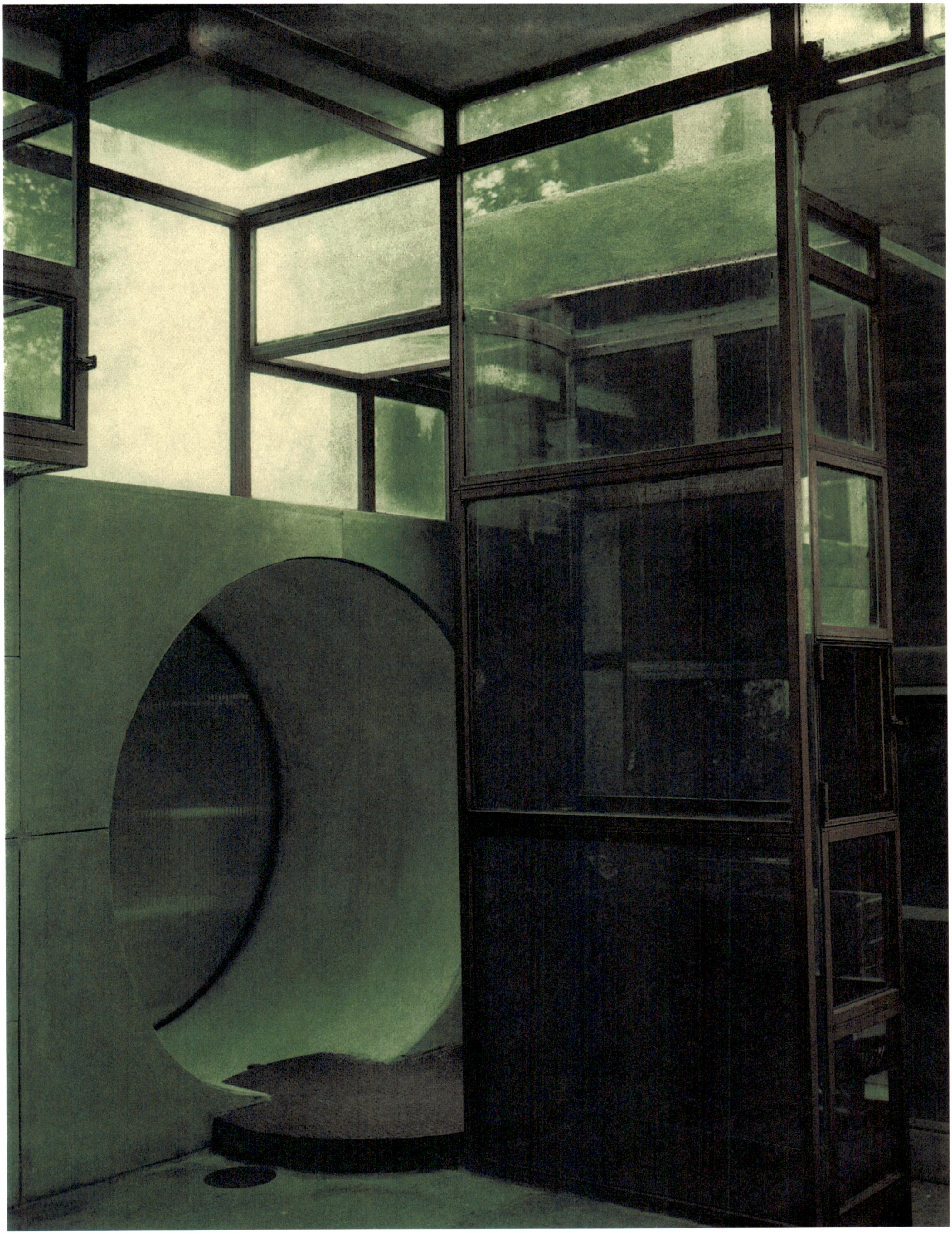

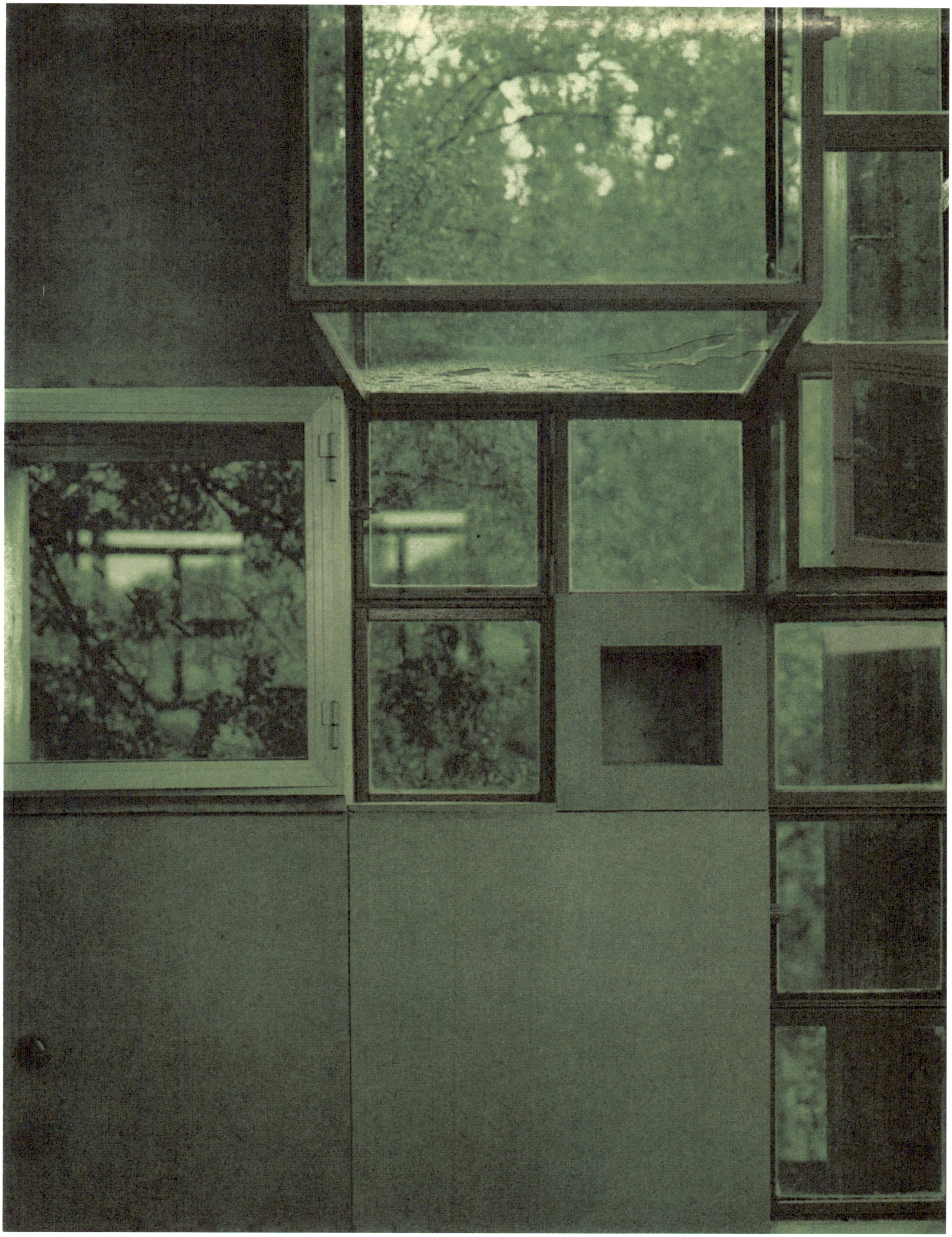

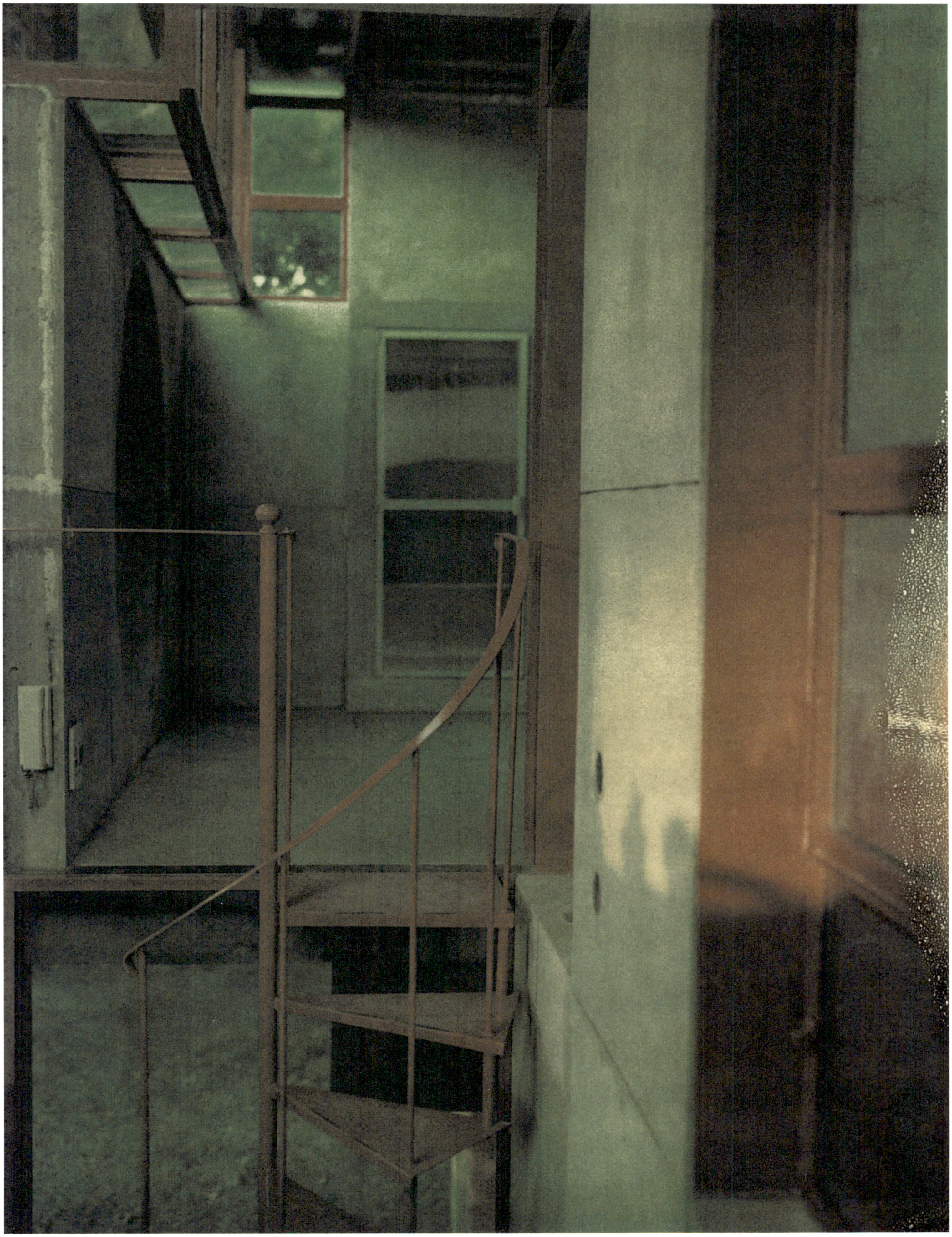

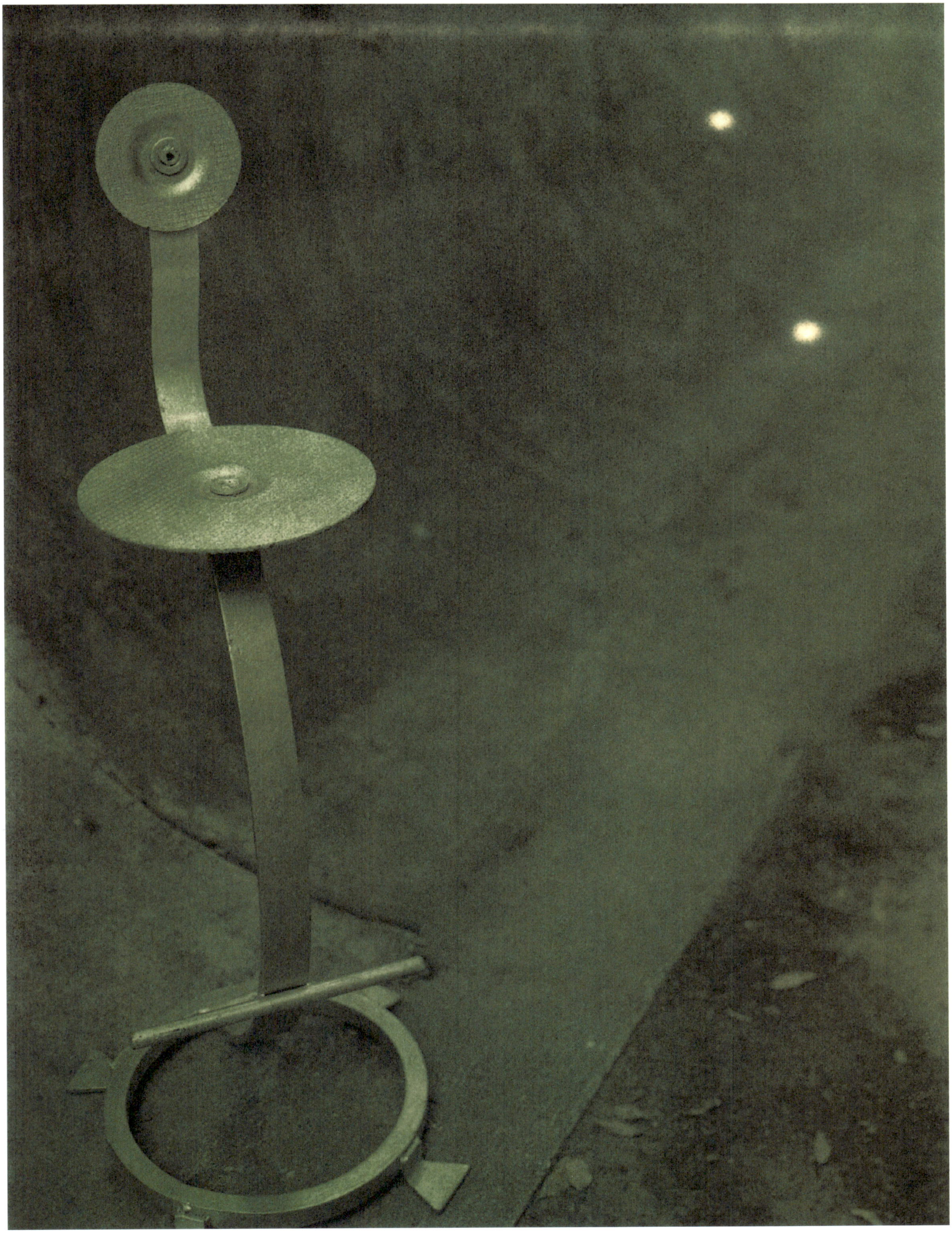

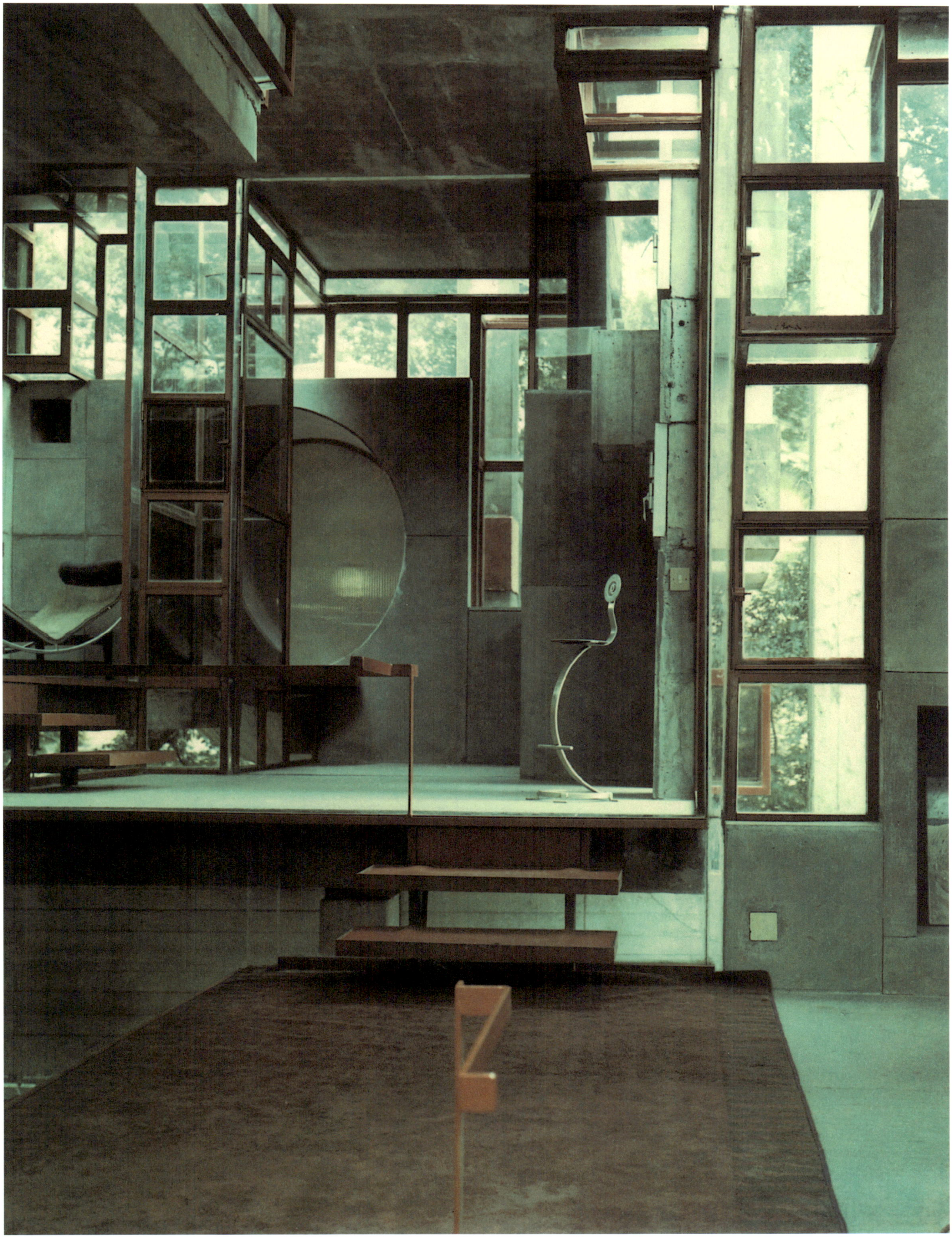

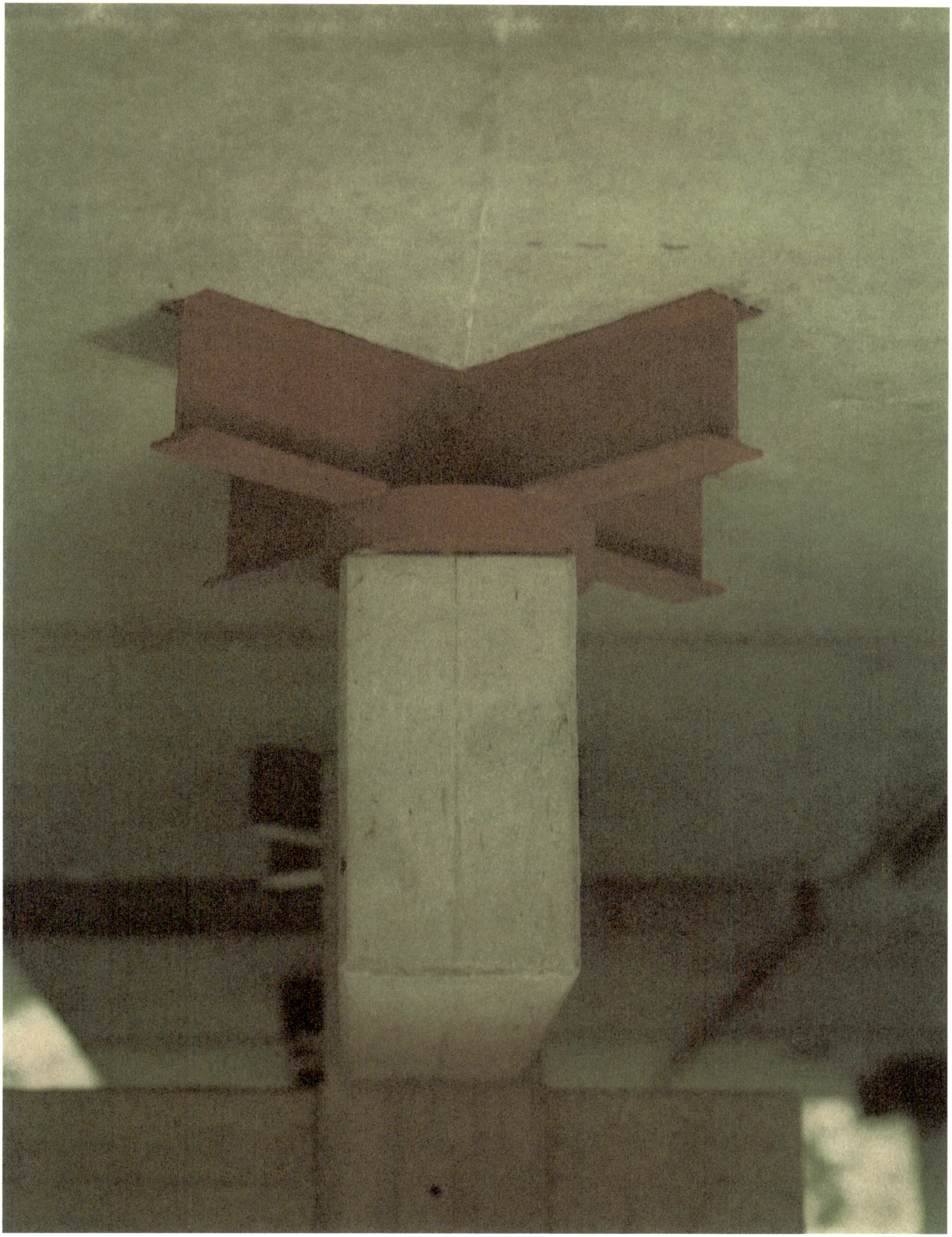

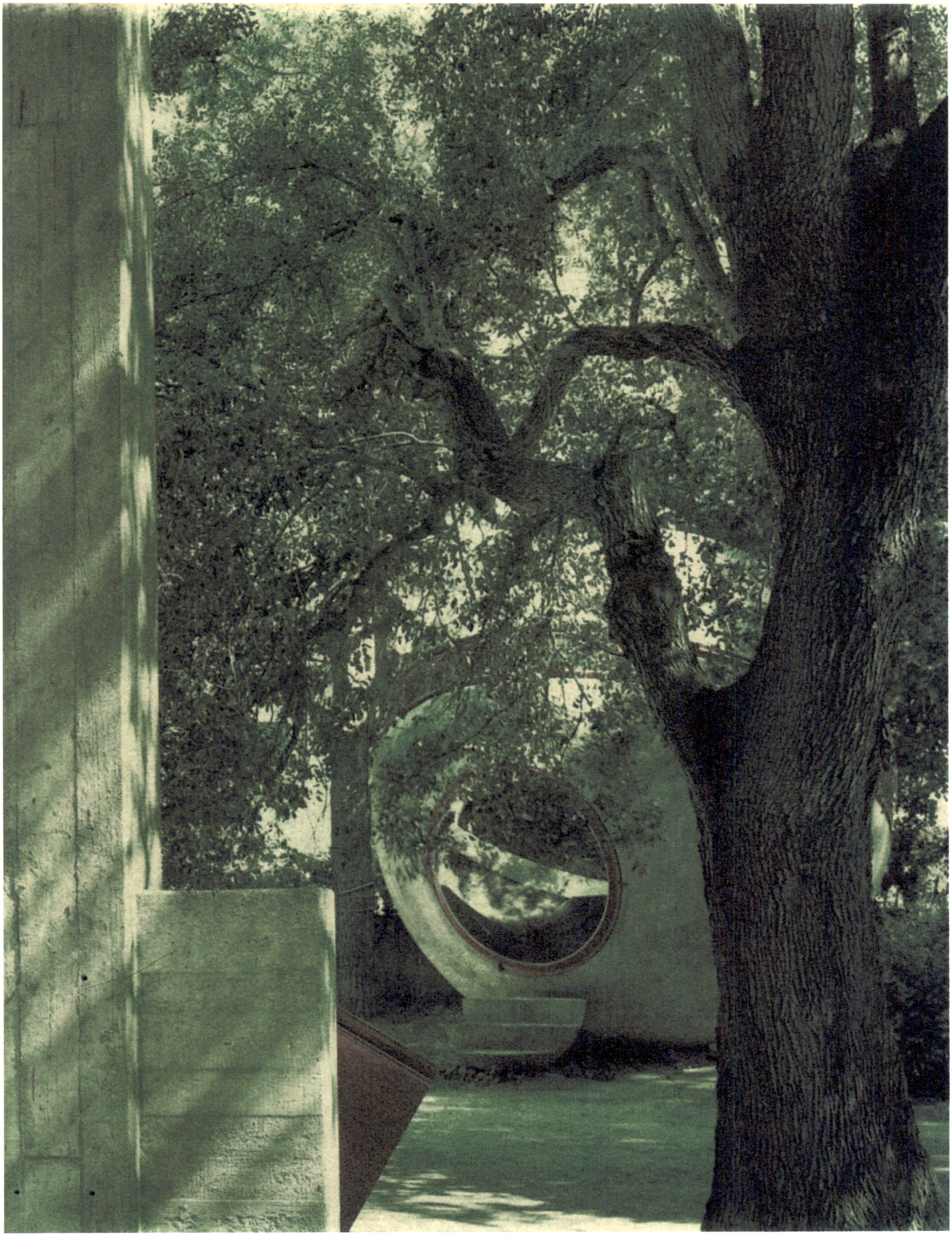

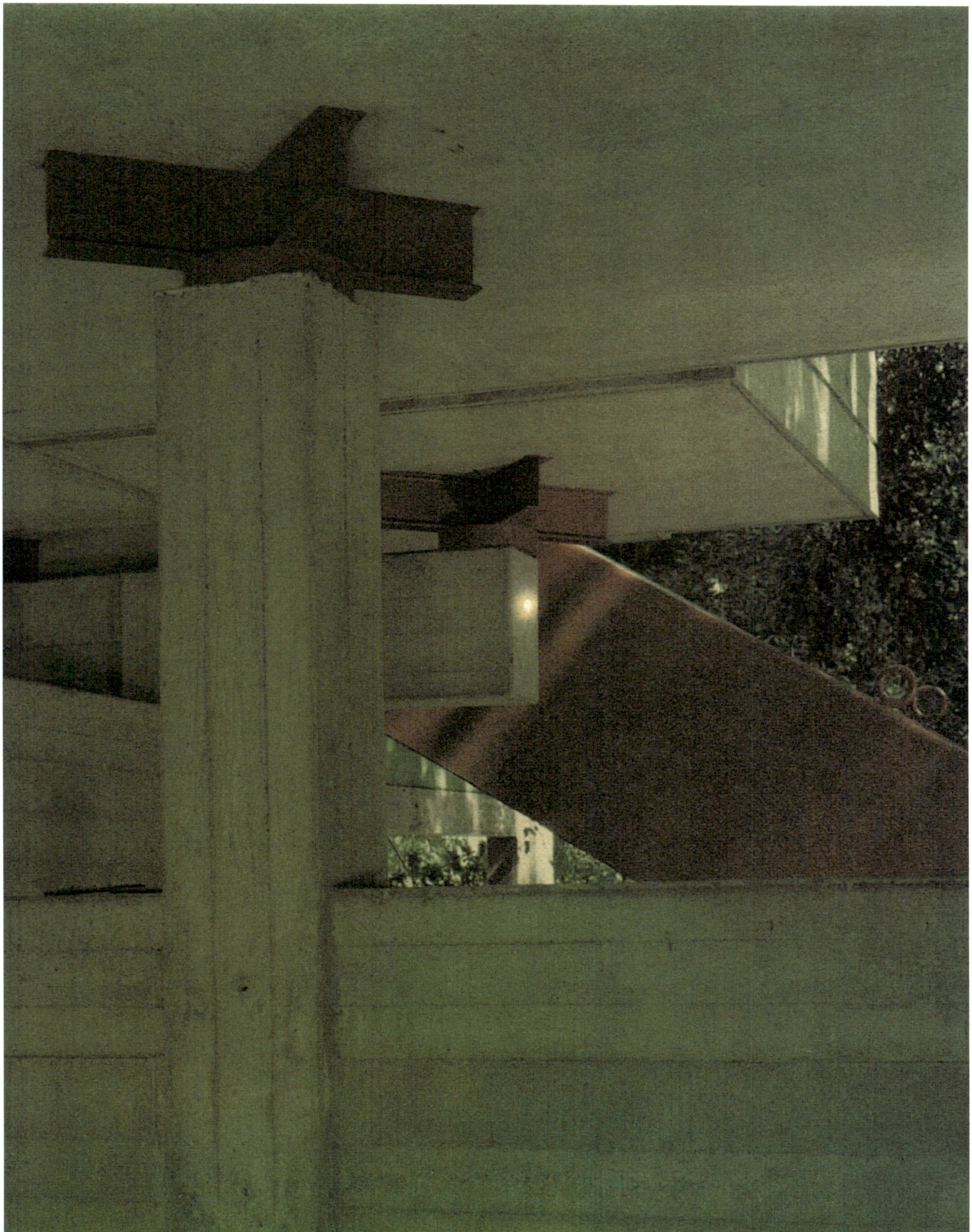

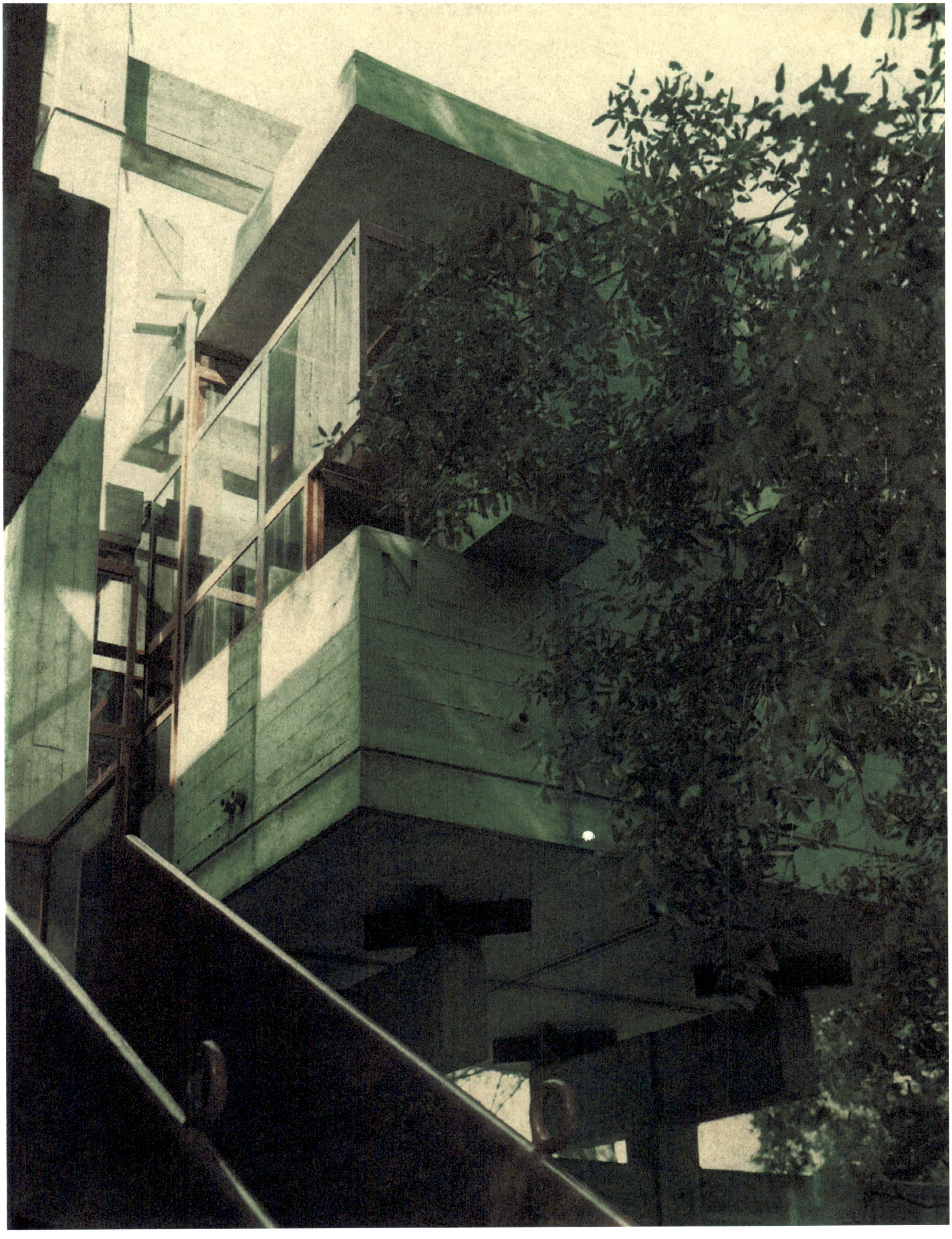

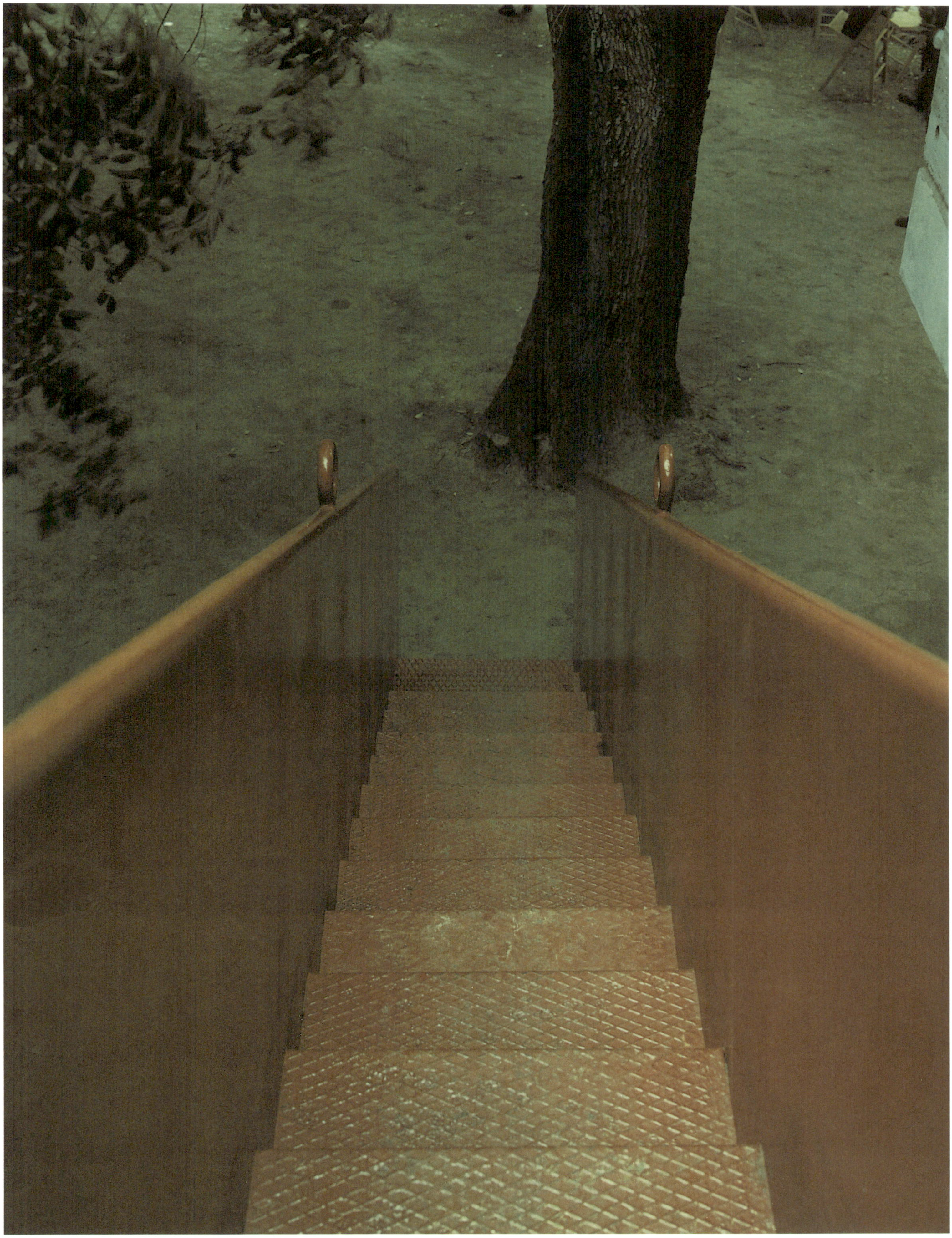

II

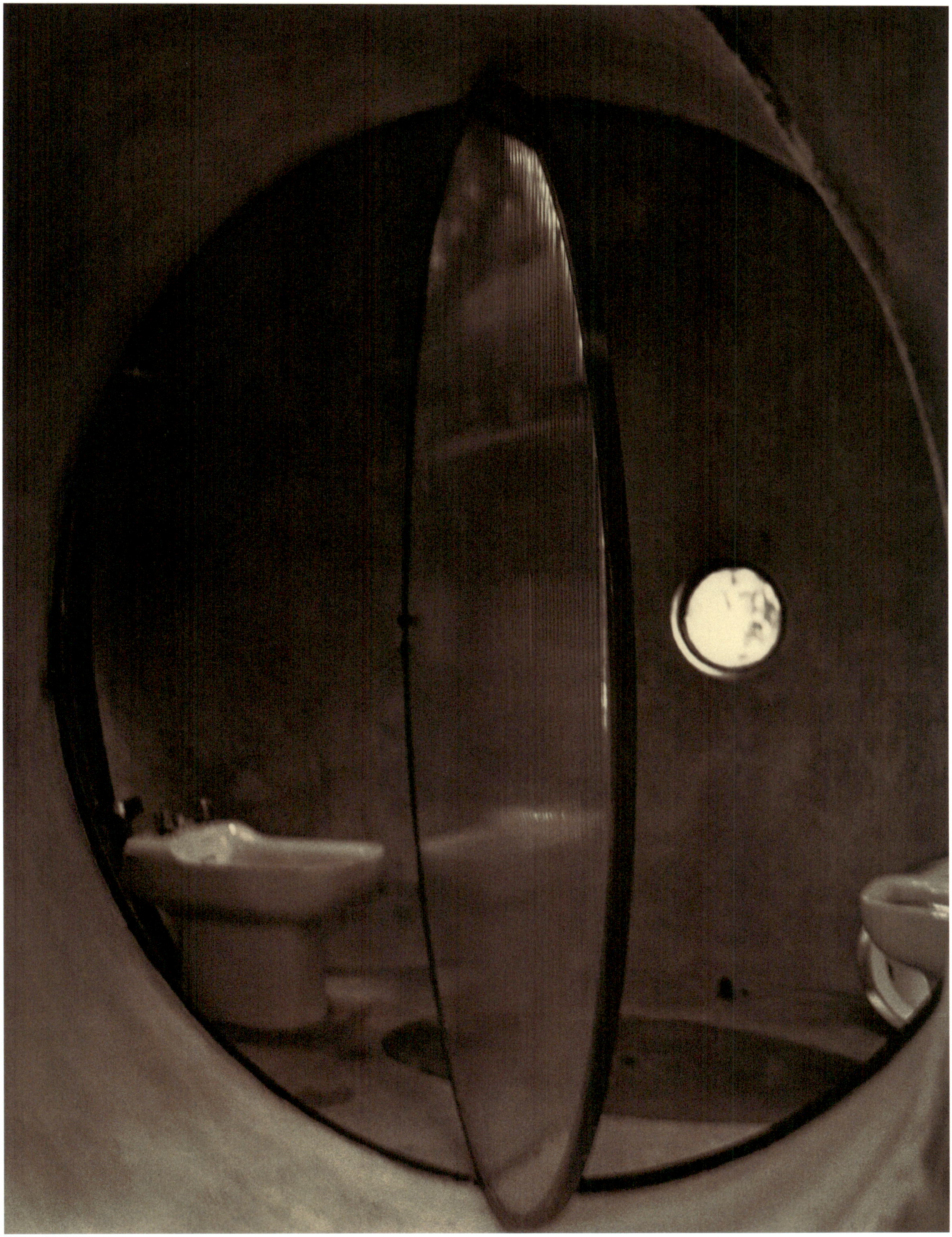

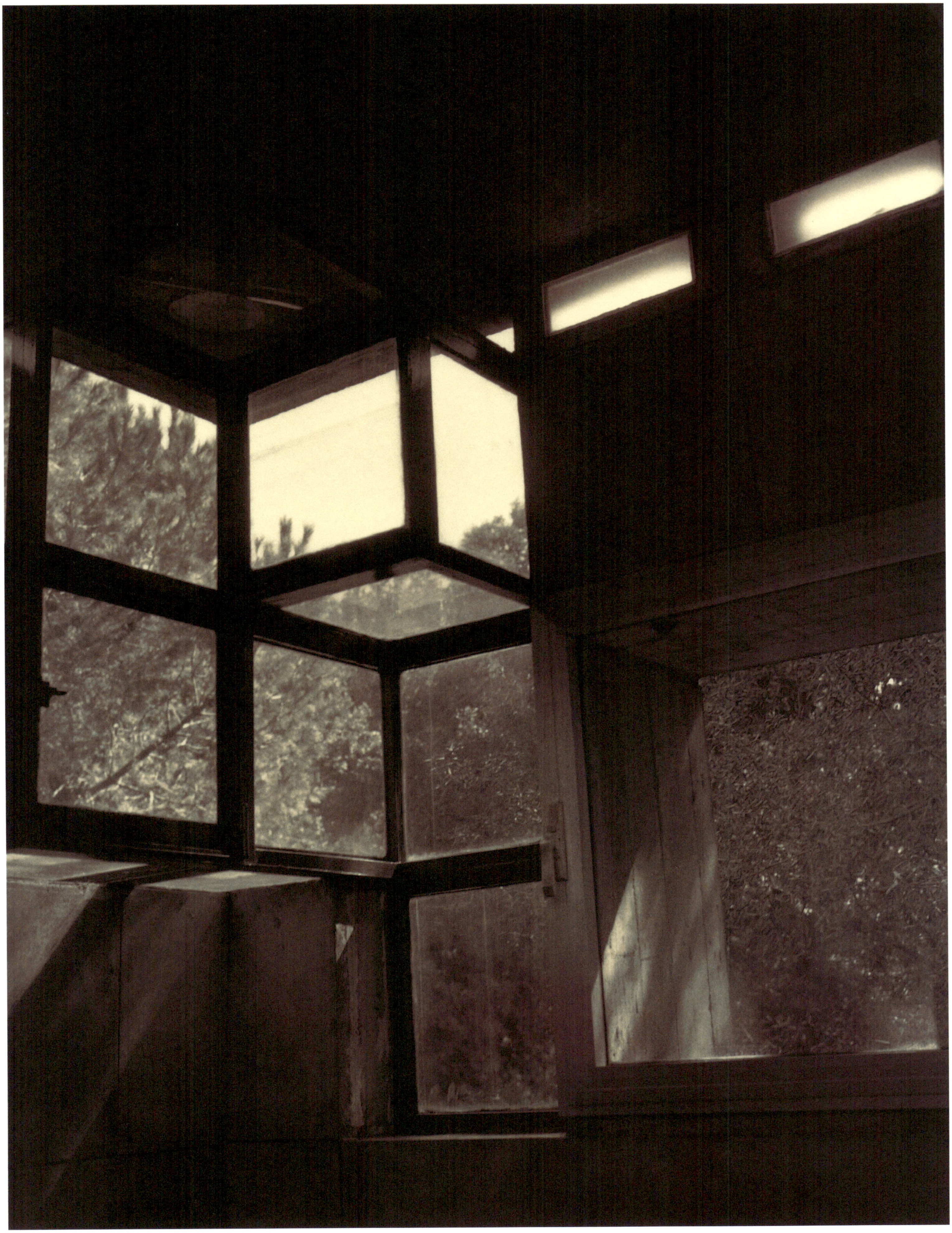

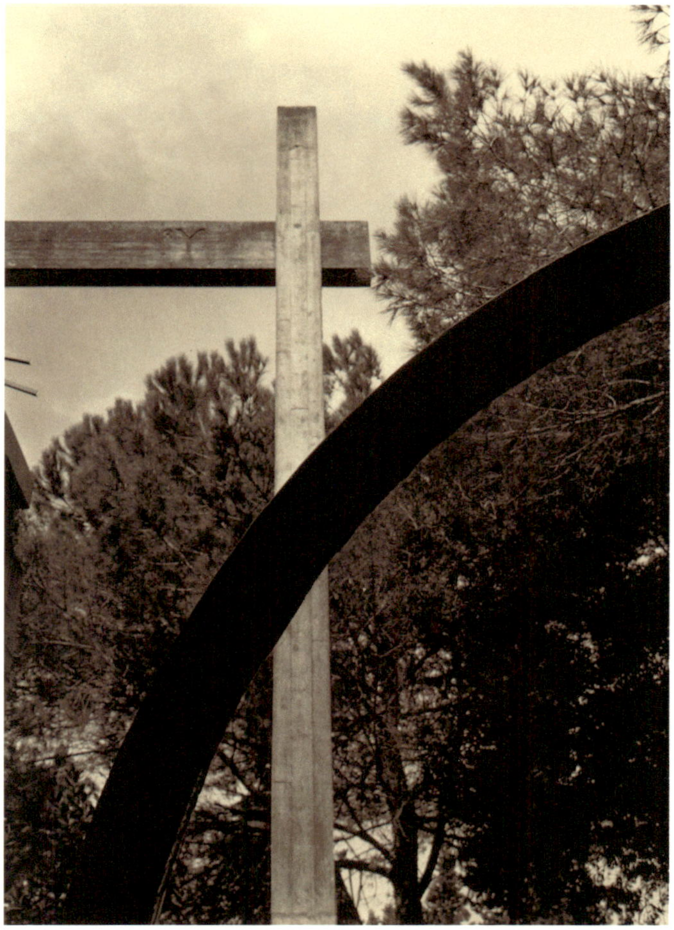
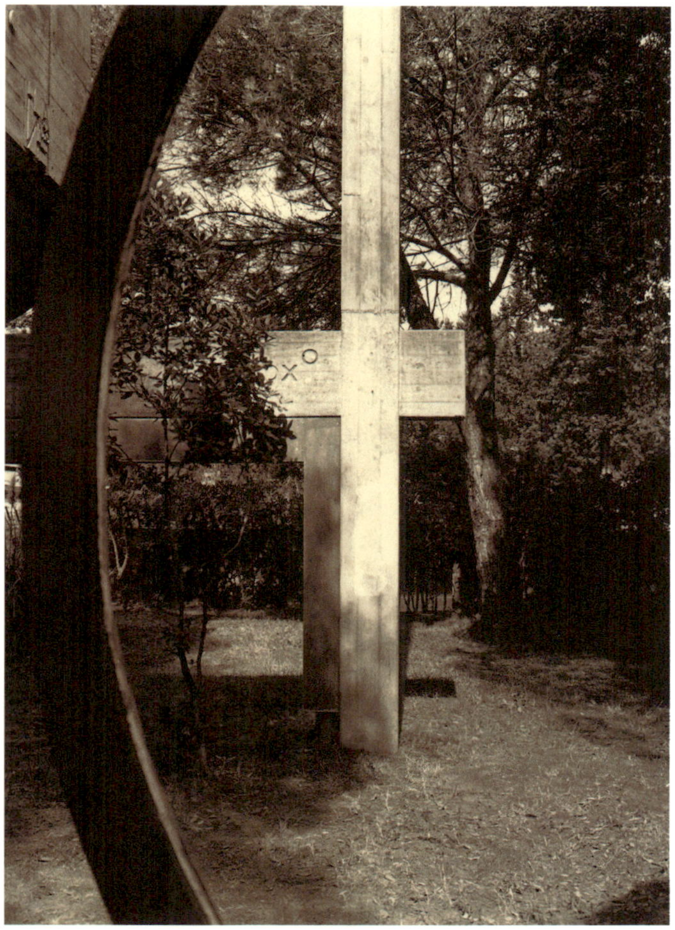
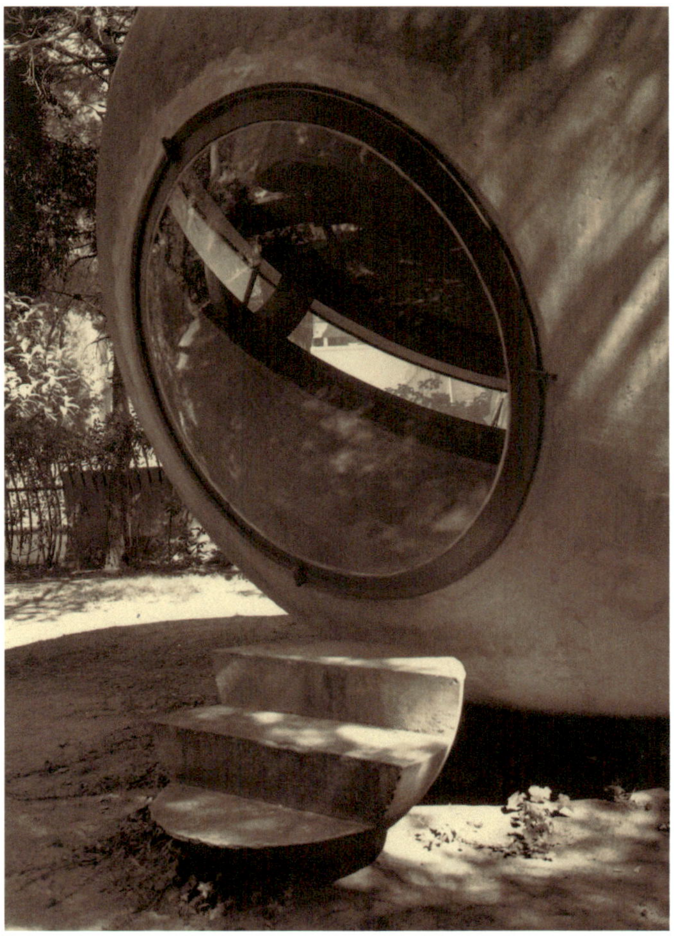
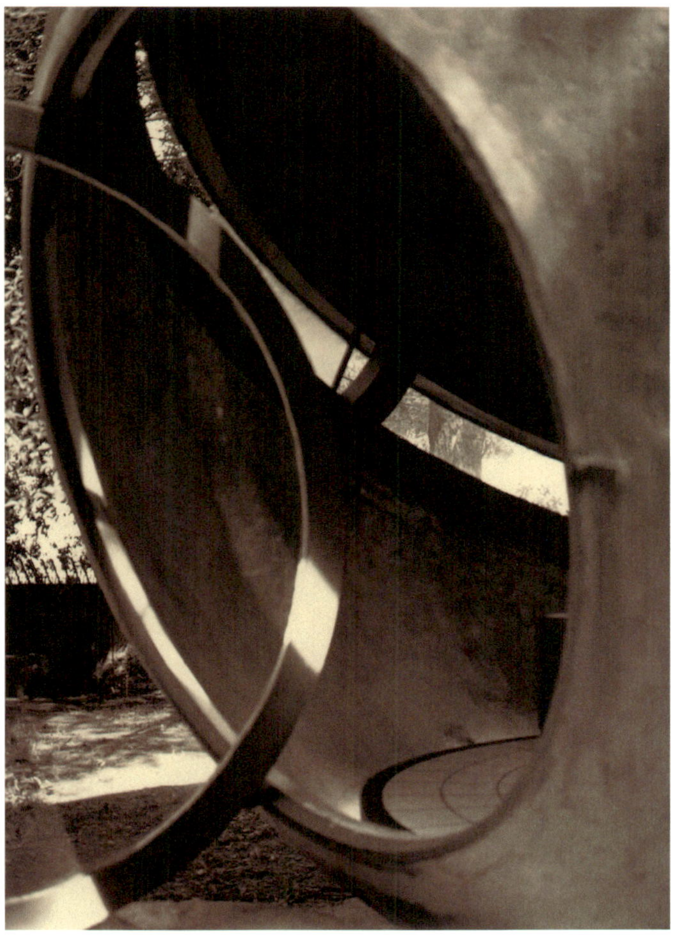

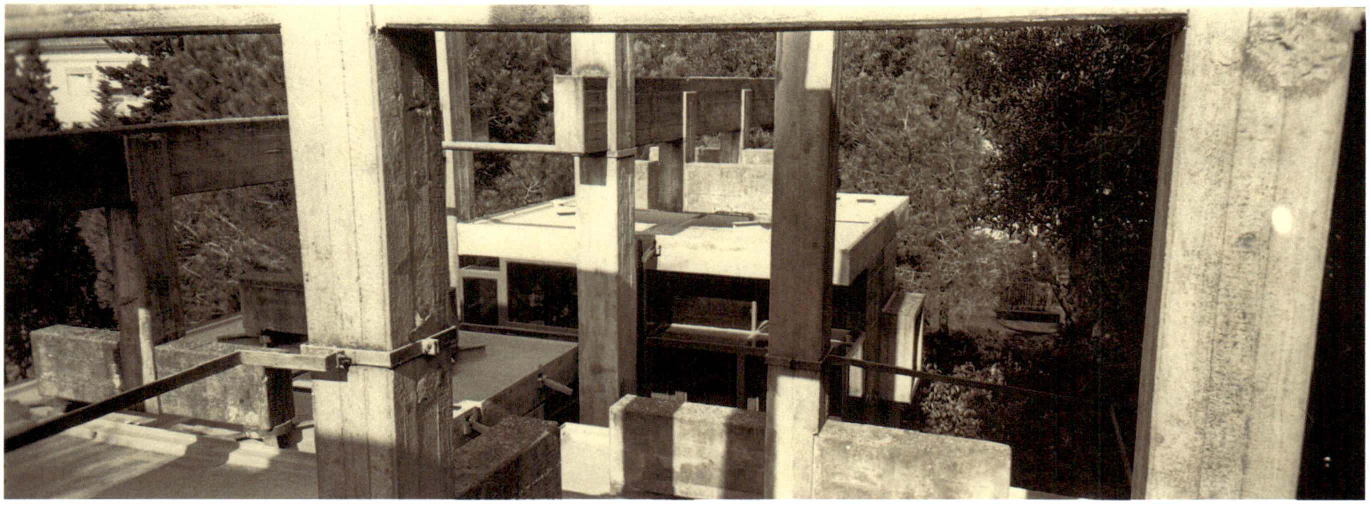
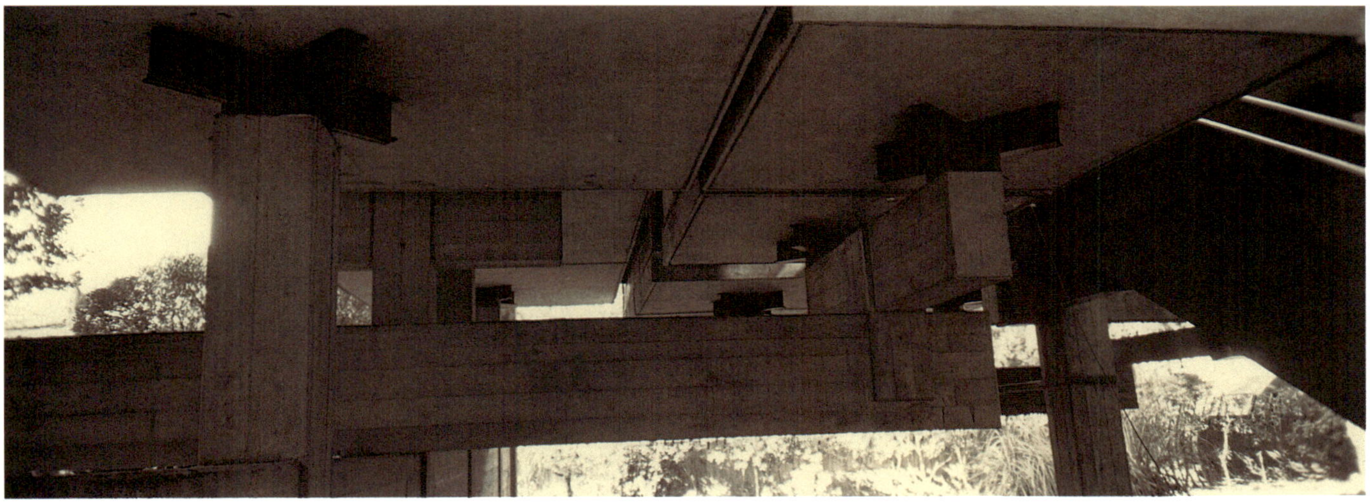
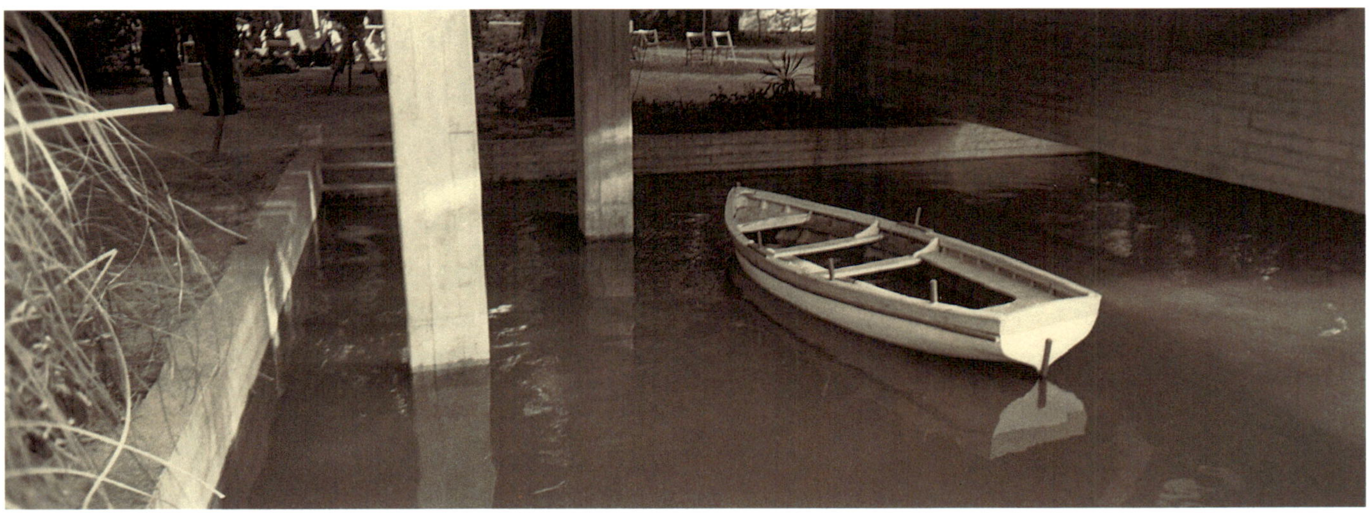

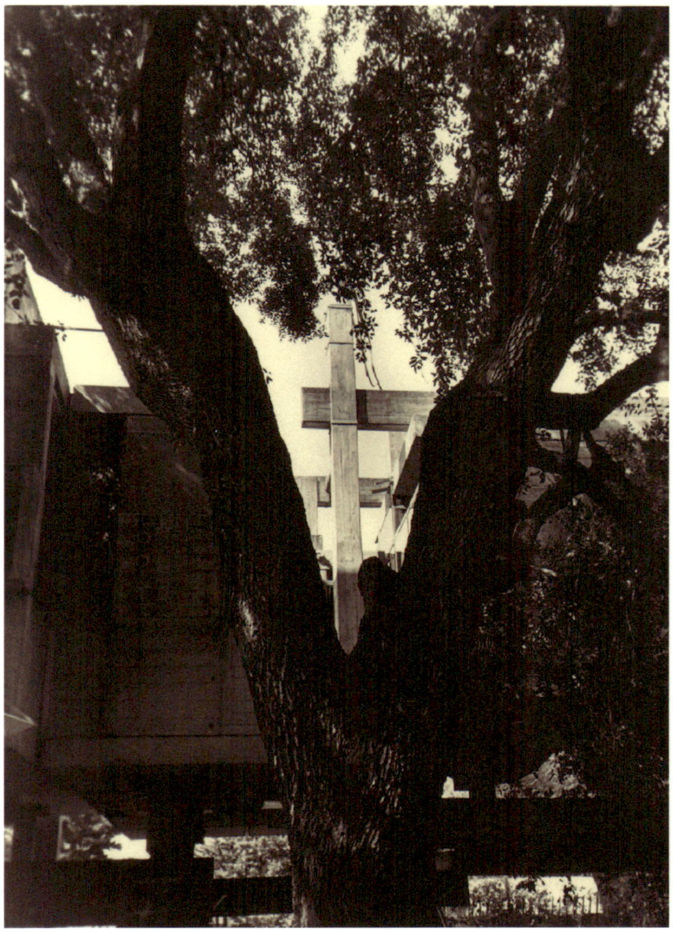
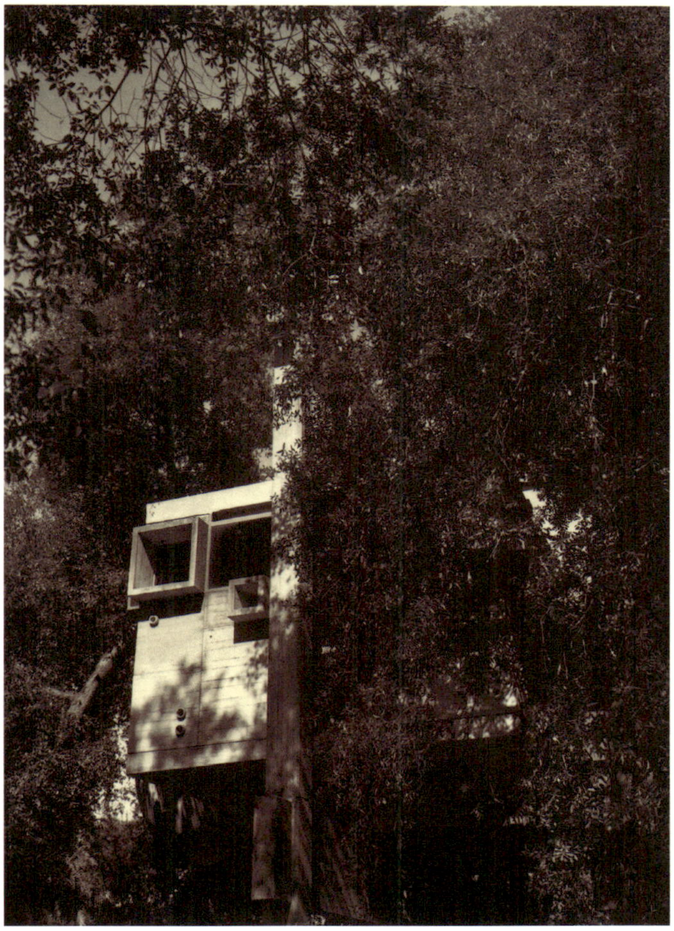
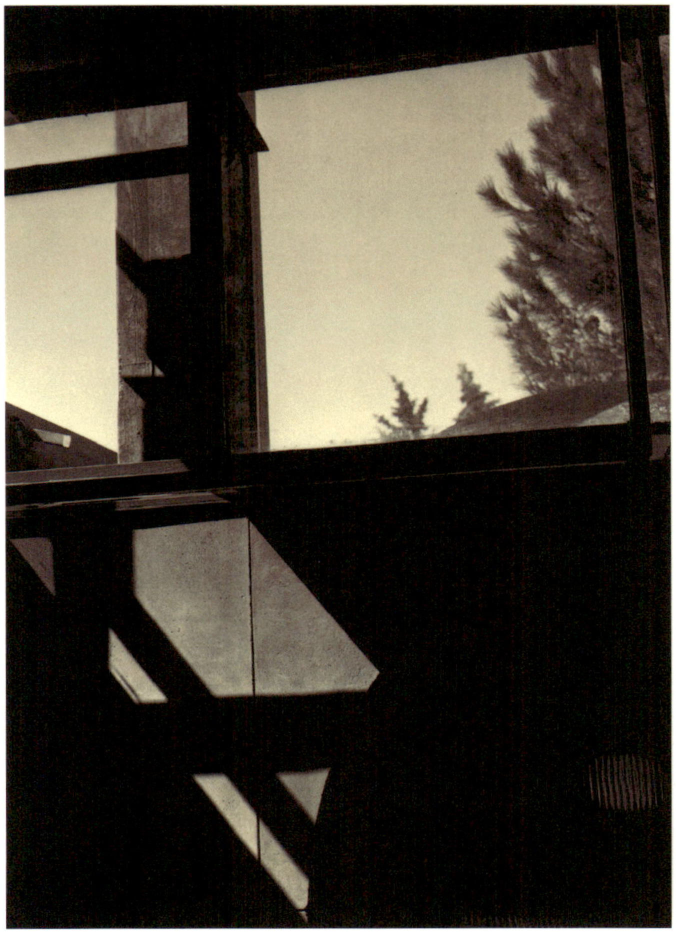
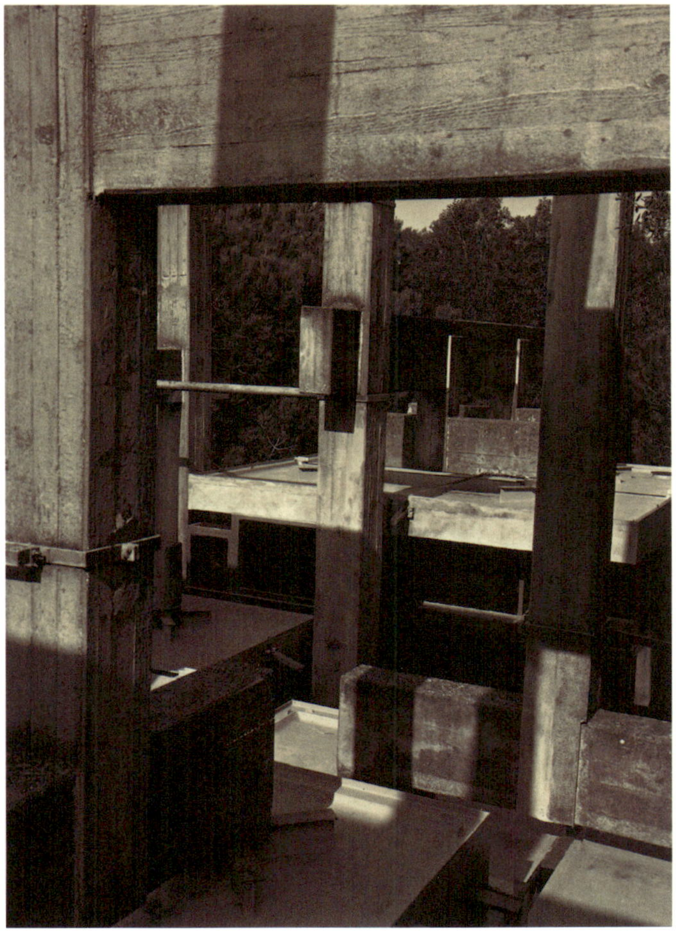

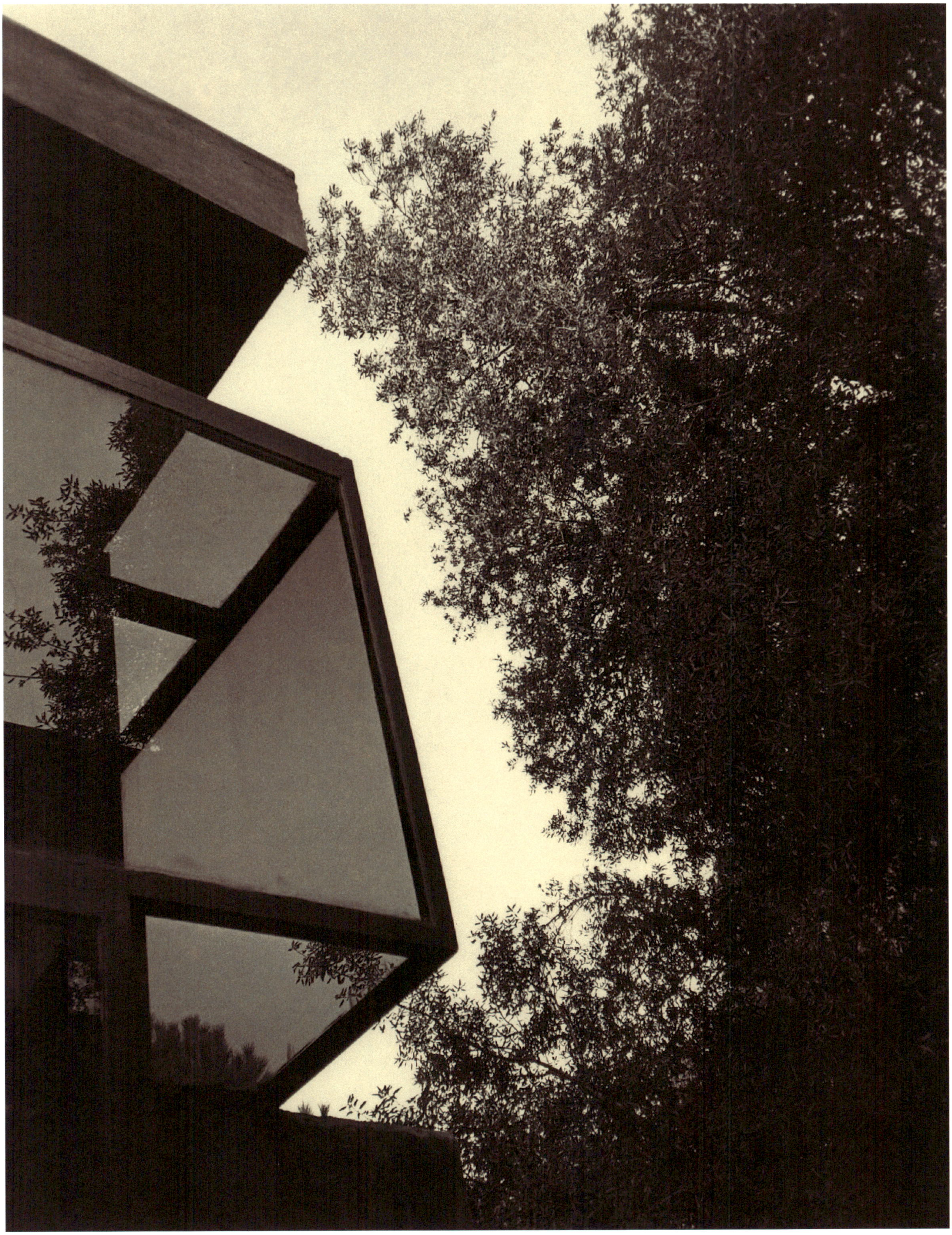

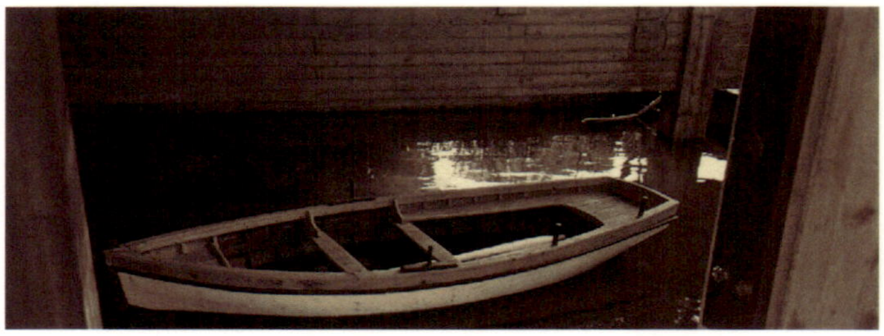

»Casa Albero nella Pineta di Fregene«
1968

The »House in the Trees« wanted to be a farewell to the normal drawing-room-bedroom house. It was an architect's dream to change the behaviour of men in a new world to come. The sixties were the years of hope for a glorious but unknown future. This house was supposed to be the final goodbye to the homes with wallpaper coziness and comfortable beds.
Disloyalty to any old habits was expected. The »House in the Trees« wanted to illustrate all that. It looked out for an uncertain tomorrow without foreseeing today's life.
This building dedicated to the future is finally only the remembrance of a futuristic dream. It was a struggle with Utopia.
Life was too short and times turned out to be different. I have no idea what this place must feel to live in during starless nights. But it was built for the sun and the nearby sea – I suppose. Architecture should create an essential incongruity in the environment. Where the house is located in Fregene made this a nearly impossible task.
It has elements of the encyclopedia of modern architecture. The lessons of the twenties found here 40 years later a different visual spelling and interpretation. The spirit of the Bauhaus, of Gropius and Moholy-Nagy as well as the Russian school of Rodchenko and Lissitzky are present here, but you can not classify this house. There is no other it could be compared to. It hangs in the tree and looks unafraid of its own weight. There is water under the house. And a little bark floating there gives still today the impression of a stranded shipwreck, the size of a giant toy. The red metal staircase leading to the house looks like the revisited version of some medieval castle's bascule bridge. There are easy lines and colors (red and gray only) to tell a visual story. Deliberate interferences make its design unclear, but give at the same time a stage-like touch. Perugini wanted to ignore how humans were used to or wanted to live.
But he had not enough time left to explain to the world his personal wishes and hopes. His voice was never allowed to be loud enough to be listened to outside of Italy. I only watched the place with the camera's eye. Then it is easy to forget the proper functions of a house.
No question is asked – the visual effect alone is the answer.
It failed as only success can fail. It had won a contest but the construction was never finished. All the concrete was supposed to be covered in aluminium opposed to the beautiful red paint. The aluminium was never applied, as the place stayed an unfinished puzzle of gray concrete volumes and lines of red paint on the metal structure.
Too many possibilities may reject the objective observer. But this place is a brilliant demonstration and it can easily hide the lack of down to earth needs of our spoiled standards.
Inside there are no suitable tables or chairs. One single prototype of an elegant metal chair looks like the beautiful skeleton of some unknown animal.
You can love this place because of its strangeness. The sensual and the intellectual entered here a childless union. Balance and serenity are not part of this impossible marriage. Unfinished as it is, the »House in the Trees« remains an interesting question mark.
With the few notes left the revelations of this architectual illusion will stay without a final answer. You can feel a strong love for illusions. Reality was second in life for this nearly abstract concept, unwatched or not listened to. The visual concept came first. Weather and time were not helpful or friendly to this beautiful souvenir of something that had never totally existed.

Karl Lagerfeld

Limited edition of 2500 books printed in 1998
Edited by Eric Pfrunder and Gerhard Steidl
Design: Karl Lagerfeld / Gerhard Steidl / Bernard Fischer
Reproductions: Gert Schwab / Steidl, Schwab Scantechnik
Paper: Munken Lynx, 200 g, Nordic Swan approved,
from Munkedals AB, Sweden
Printing and production: Steidl, Göttingen

Düstere Str. 4, D-37073 Göttingen
More information about the other books by Karl Lagerfeld:
http://www.steidl.de

ISBN 3-88243-648-4
Printed in Germany